Nature's Rivals

Crocodile vs. Hippopotamus

I0885749

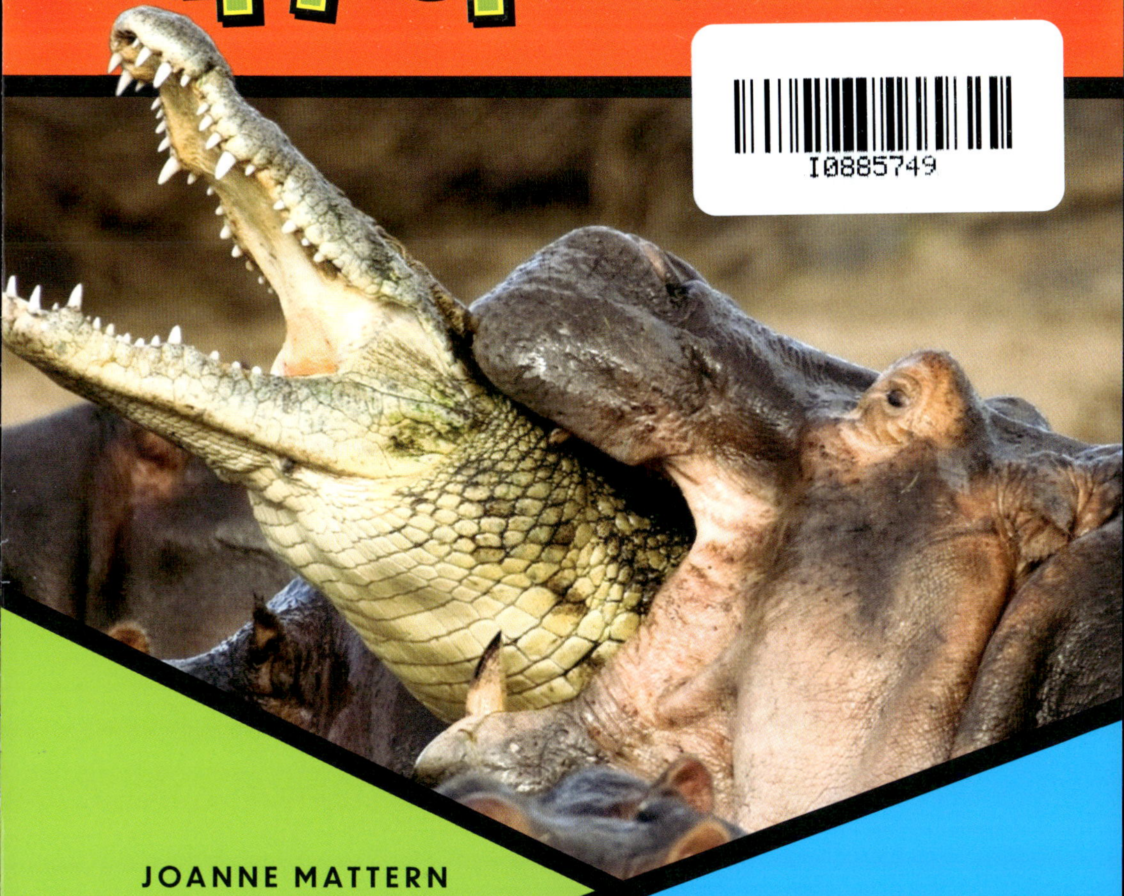

JOANNE MATTERN

Mitchell Lane
PUBLISHERS

Parent and Caregiver Tips for Creating Nonfiction Readers

The high-interest topics in the *Nature's Rivals* series are sure to get your young reader excited about reading nonfiction. While exploring a fascinating subject, your reader will be introduced to new concepts, facts, ideas, and vocabulary.

Tips for Reading Nonfiction

Talk about Nonfiction

Explain that nonfiction books provide facts about real-world topics. When readers read nonfiction, they gain a rich understanding of the world. They build background knowledge that provides a foundation for learning and academic success.

Look at the Parts

This book contains the following helpful features. Share the purpose of each feature with your reader.

Photos, Captions, and Graphic Aids

The photos, captions, charts, maps, and other graphic aids in nonfiction texts contain a wealth of information. Help your reader identify different ways information can be displayed.

Sidebars

These extra tidbits of information help satisfy readers' curiosity and expand their knowledge.

Table of Contents

Located at the front of the book, this list shows the big ideas within the text and the page numbers where they can be found.

Glossary

Located at the back of the book, the glossary defines key words and phrases that are related to the topic. These words and phrases can be found in the text in **bold** type.

Comprehension Questions (Fact Check)

Multiple-choice questions help readers self-check to make sure they understand what they read.

Index

Located at the back of the book, the index is an alphabetical list of topics and the page numbers where they can be found.

With a little help and guidance, your reader will be on their way to enjoying and learning from nonfiction books.

Mitchell Lane
PUBLISHERS

mitchelllanepub.com

2001 SW 31st Avenue
Hallandale, FL 33009

Copyright © 2026 by Mitchell Lane Publishers. All rights reserved. No part of this book may be reproduced without written permission from the publisher. Printed and bound in the United States of America.

First Edition, 2026.
Author: Joanne Mattern
Designer: Jen Bowers
Editor: Tricia Hoffman

Series: Nature's Rivals
Title: Crocodile vs. Hippopotamus / by Joanne Mattern

Hallandale, FL : Mitchell Lane Publishers, [2026]

Library bound ISBN: 979-8-89260-599-1
Paperback ISBN: 979-8-89260-611-0
eBook ISBN: 979-8-89260-610-3

PHOTO CREDITS
Alamy: Barbara von Hoffmann, 25; Media Drum World, 25; Shutterstock: FADIL YOUNESS, cover and 1; Brian Stuart Nel, 3; Jean-Marc Pierard, 4, Melnikov Dmitriy, 4; tantrik71, 5; Henk Bogaard, 6, Speedshutter, 6; Etienne Outram, 7; Martin Pelanek, 8, 28; BEST BACKGROUNDS, 9, Supriyo Ghoshal, 9; Butterflies on the wall, 10; Mieke Suharini, 11, MAHATHIR MOHD YASIN, 11; Dogholiday, 12; Michiel de Wit, 13, David Sharman Dunkley, 13; PhotocechcZ, 14; Dafna Ben nun, 15; asharkyu, 16; Jacktamrong, 17, e2dan, 17; Tatiana Grozetskaya, 18; all latitudes, 19; nwdph, 20, 28; Nick Greaves, 21; Stephen Lew, 22, WICHAN KONGCHAN, 22; Me dia, 23, Goldquest, 23; DW34, 24; bigiom jom, 25; Glumchameleon, 26; salimreza 1989, 27, Zoltan Tarlacz, 27; Peter Hermes Furian, 28

Contents

Wetland War

The Nile crocodile is hungry. He prowls the long grass near the river, looking for easy **prey**. A herd of hippos **grazes** nearby. But the crocodile knows better than to attack an adult hippopotamus. Hippos are much too big and strong for the crocodile to kill.

The crocodile spots a hippo calf that has wandered too far from its mother. Adult hippos are too dangerous, but a baby is another story. The crocodile creeps through the grass, moving closer and closer to his target.

The mother hippopotamus has spotted the danger to her calf. She runs toward the crocodile. But the crocodile is hungry. He stands his ground.

The hippo opens her mouth wide. She tries to bite the crocodile with her long, sharp teeth. The crocodile heads back to the river. The hippo chases him. Both animals disappear under the water. What will happen next?

Crocodiles Rule

Nile crocodiles are fierce **predators**. These huge beasts are the second largest **reptile** on Earth. A Nile croc can weigh between 500 and 900 pounds (226 and 408 kg) and measure almost 10 feet (3 meters) long.

Nile crocs live in **wetlands** in Africa. Like crocodiles in other parts of the world, these animals always live near water. They are excellent swimmers. A crocodile can swim as fast as 15 miles (24 km) per hour.

The World's Biggest

The largest reptile on Earth is another crocodile, called the saltwater crocodile.

Crocodiles are carnivores that eat many other animals. Crocs are **ambush** hunters. They sneak up on their prey. Then, they grab the prey in their powerful jaws. Their teeth rip off chunks of flesh.

Is there anything a crocodile won't eat? Not really. These bad boys will prey on just about anything that moves, including fish, pigs, deer, and even big cats.

Watch Out!

Crocodiles often drown their prey by rolling over to trap the animal under water. This move is called a death roll.

A crocodile's jaw is amazingly powerful. Once it closes around an animal, its prey has no chance to escape. That's because a croc's jaws can bite down with tremendous pressure. A croc can easily crush a turtle's shell or a pig's skull with one chomp.

A crocodile also has many sharp teeth. These teeth can grip an animal so it can't escape the deadly bite.

Open Wide

It's almost impossible to open a croc's jaws, but a person can hold the animal's jaws closed with one hand. That's because the muscles that open a croc's jaws are weak, but the ones that close it are very strong.

Hippo Power

Hippopotamuses are one of the largest **mammals** on Earth. A male hippo can weigh more than 9,000 pounds (4,000 kg). These big boys can be up to 16 feet (4.5 meters) long. They stand more than five feet (1.5 meters) tall at the shoulder.

Hippos aren't just big. They are powerful! Their heavy bodies can crush an enemy. You don't want a hippo to sit on you!

What's in a Name?

The word "hippopotamus" comes from an ancient Greek word meaning "water horse."

Let's talk teeth. A hippo has 36 teeth. That's a lot fewer than a crocodile, but a hippo's teeth are bigger ... much bigger! Some of a hippo's teeth can be up to 20 inches (50 cm) long. That's about as long as the pillow on your bed. And a hippo can open its mouth up to four feet (1.2 meters) wide. That's about as tall as you! A big mouth full of big teeth makes the hippo a deadly enemy.

Crush!

A hippo's bite is three times stronger than a lion's.

Hippos spend most of their time in the water. That's because they need to keep their skin wet. If a hippo is on land for too long, it will become **dehydrated**. But even though hippos love the water, their bodies are too heavy to swim. Hippos don't float, they sink! These big animals walk along the bottom of the river instead of swimming.

Hippos also love to wallow in the mud. The mud keeps the hippo cool. It also prevents insects from biting the hippo's thick skin.

Hippopotamuses are herbivores. They only eat plants. Hippos leave the river at night to graze on grass that grows near the water. They eat fruit that falls from trees too.

Hippos live in big groups. A herd of hippos stays in the same **territory**. They don't like intruders and will fight other animals that come into their area.

A Stinky Space

Hippos mark their territories by spraying the area with their poop.

The Battle is On

Let's get back to our crocodile and hippopotamus battle. When we last saw them, the animals had headed into the river. The crocodile is a good swimmer and could easily get away from the hippo. But the hippo catches the croc and bites down hard on his tail.

The hippo's bite doesn't do any damage. That's because the crocodile is covered with thick **scales** that protect him from injury. The hippo tries again. She opens her huge mouth. But she is too late. The croc has disappeared.

Or has he? The crocodile swims back to the hippo and chomps down on the bigger animal's leg. The croc's sharp teeth bite through the hippo's skin. The hippo crawls backward. Blood stains the water.

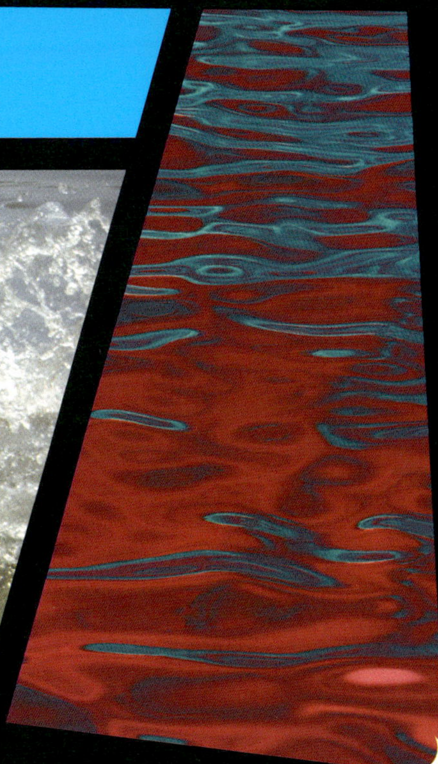

But the hippo is still fighting. She opens her mouth again and tries to catch the faster crocodile in her huge teeth. If she does, it could be all over for the croc.

What will happen next? Think about each animal's weapons and defenses. Then, decide who you think will win this deadly battle!

Crocodile vs. Hippopotamus

Range of Nile Crocodile

Range of Hippopotamus

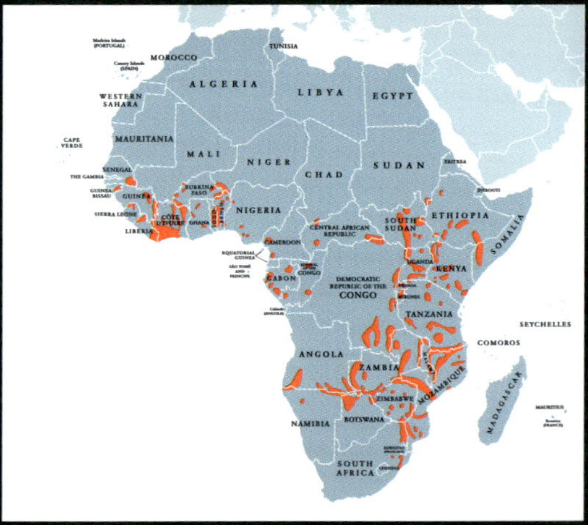

Let's Compare

Size

Crocodile: Weight—500 to 900 pounds (226 to 408 kg); Length—up to 10 feet (3 meters)

Hippo: Weight—More than 9,000 pounds (4,000 kg); Length—up to 16 feet (4.5 meters)

Teeth

Crocodile: 64 to 68 small, sharp teeth

Hippo: 36 long, sharp teeth

Weapons

Crocodile: Powerful bite, sharp teeth, strong tail, powerful muscles

Hippo: Long teeth, big mouth, heavy body

Defenses

Crocodile: Moves fast on land and water, has thick scales, able to **camouflage** itself in water and on land

Hippo: Moves fast on land, heavy body, thick skin

Glossary

ambush (AM-bush)
a surprise attack from a hidden animal

camouflage (KAM-uh-flahzh)
to disguise something so that it blends in with its surroundings

dehydrated (dee-HYE-dray-tid)
when the body loses a large amount of water

grazes (GRAZEZ)
eats grass in a field

mammals (MAM-uhlz)
animals that are warm-blooded, have hair or fur, and nurse their babies

predators (PRED-uh-turz)
animals that eat other animals

prey (PRAY)
an animal that is hunted by another animal for food

reptile (REP-tile)
an animal that is cold-blooded, has scales, and lays eggs

scales (SKALEZ)
thin, flat, overlapping pieces of hard skin that cover a reptile's body

territory (TER-i-tor-ee)
the area where an animal lives

wetlands (WET-landz)
land that is covered by water most of the time

Fact Check

1. Crocodiles and hippos both live near ______.
   A. mountains B. water C. forests

2. A crocodile has powerful ______.
   A. jaws B. claws C. legs

3. Hippos are too heavy to ______.
   A. run B. swim C. attack

4. A crocodile's ______ protect it from harm.
   A. mouth B. tail C. scales

Answers
1. B, 2. A, 3. B, 4. C

Further Reading

BOOKS

Downs, Kieran. *Nile Crocodile vs. Hippopotamus*. Bellwether Media, 2021.

Klepinger, Teresa. *Crocodile vs. Hippo*. Kaleidoscope, 2022.

Roggio, Sarah. *Crocodiles vs. Hippos: Food Chain Fights*. Lerner Publications, 2024.

ON THE INTERNET

Britannica Kids: Nile Crocodile
kids.britannica.com/kids/article/Nile-crocodile/602169
Check out more about the Nile crocodile, including where it lives, what it looks like, and fun facts.

National Geographic Kids: 10 Hippo Facts!
www.natgeokids.com/uk/discover/animals/general-animals/ten-hippo-facts/
Learn even more about hippos with these 10 fascinating facts.

Index

About the Author

Joanne Mattern has written many nonfiction books for children. She adores animals of all kinds but has a special place in her heart for reptiles like the crocodile. She would love to witness a battle between a croc and a hippo, but has only seen both animals in zoos, which are some of her favorite places to visit. Joanne lives in New York State with her family, where there are no crocs or hippos to battle it out in her neighborhood.